Charles-Auguste de BÉRIOT

(1802 – 1870)

Concerto No. 9 for Violin and Orchestra, Op. 104
A minor / la mineur / a-moll

Edited by
Herbert Scherz

DOWANI International

Preface

Charles-Auguste de Bériot was a Belgian violinist, teacher, and composer whose principal works included ten concertos for the violin. This *DOWANI 3 Tempi Play Along* edition allows you to learn Bériot's Concerto No. 9 in A minor for violin and orchestra at three different tempi with professional accompaniment. It is a revised new edition in which, among other things, fingering marks have been added to the solo part.

The first CD (CD A) opens with the concert version of each movement (violin and orchestra). After tuning your instrument (Track 1 on both CDs), the musical work can begin. First, you will hear the piano accompaniment at slow tempo (CD A) and medium tempo (CD B) for practice purposes. At slow tempo you can also hear the violin played softly in the background as a guide. Having mastered these levels, you can now play the piece with orchestra at the original tempo (CD B). Each movement has been sensibly divided into subsections for practice purposes. You can select the subsection you want using the track numbers indicated in the solo part. Further explanations can be found at the end of this volume along with the names of the musicians involved in the recording. More detailed information can be found in the Internet at www.dowani.com. All of the versions were recorded live.

The fingering and bowing marks in our volume were provided by Herbert Scherz, a renowned violin teacher who for many years was professor of violin and violin methodology at the conservatories in Lucerne and Zurich. Today, after his retirement, he continues to teach very successfully on a private basis. His pupils have won more than 150 prizes at violin and chamber music competitions; many of them now have successful international careers. In 1985 he founded the "Lucerne Ministrings", an ensemble of children and teenagers up to the age of 16 that has given many concerts in Switzerland and abroad.

We wish you lots of fun playing from our *DOWANI 3 Tempi Play Along* editions and hope that your musicality and diligence will enable you to play the concert version as soon as possible. Our goal is to provide the essential conditions you need for effective practicing through motivation, enjoyment and fun.

Your DOWANI Team

Avant-propos

Charles-Auguste de Bériot fut un violoniste, pédagogue et compositeur belge. Les dix concertos pour violon font partie de ses œuvres principales. La présente édition de la collection *DOWANI 3 Tempi Play Along* vous permet de travailler son concerto n° 9 pour violon et orchestre en la mineur d'une manière systématique dans trois différents tempos avec un accompagnement professionnel. Il s'agit d'une édition révisée avec, entre autres, une nouvelle partie soliste avec doigtés.

Le premier CD (CD A) vous permettra d'entendre d'abord la version de concert de chaque mouvement (violon et orchestre). Après avoir accordé votre instrument (sur les deux CDs plage n° 1), vous pourrez commencer le travail musical. Pour travailler le morceau au tempo lent (CD A) et au tempo moyen (CD B), vous entendrez l'accompagnement de piano. Au tempo lent, le violon restera cependant toujours audible très doucement à l'arrière-plan. Vous pourrez ensuite jouer le tempo original (CD B) avec accompagnement d'orchestre. Chaque mouvement a été divisé en sections judicieuses pour faciliter le travail. Vous pouvez sélectionner ces sections à l'aide des numéros de plages indiqués dans la partie du soliste. Pour obtenir plus d'informations et les noms des artistes qui ont participé aux enregistrements, veuillez consulter la dernière page de cette édition ou notre site Internet : www.dowani.com. Toutes les versions ont été enregistrées en direct.

Les doigtés et indications des coups d'archet proviennent de Herbert Scherz, violoniste et pédagogue de grande renommée. Il fut pendant de nombreuses années professeur de violon et de la méthodique de violon aux Conservatoires Supérieures de Musique à Lucerne et Zurich et donne depuis sa retraite toujours des cours privés avec grand succès. Ses élèves ont reçus plus de 150 prix aux concours de violon et de musique de chambre et beaucoup d'entre eux ont du succès au niveau international. En

1985, il fonda les "Ministrings Luzern", un ensemble d'enfants et de jeunes jusqu'à 16 ans qui donne de nombreux concerts en Suisse et à l'étranger.

Nous vous souhaitons beaucoup de plaisir à faire de la musique avec la collection *DOWANI 3 Tempi Play Along* et nous espérons que votre musicalité et votre application vous amèneront aussi rapidement que possible à la version de concert. Notre but est de vous offrir les bases nécessaires pour un travail efficace par la motivation et le plaisir.

Les Éditions DOWANI

Vorwort

Charles-Auguste de Bériot war ein belgischer Violinist, Violinpädagoge und Komponist. Zu seinen Hauptwerken gehören zehn Violinkonzerte. Mit Hilfe der vorliegenden *DOWANI 3 Tempi Play Along*-Ausgabe können Sie Bériots Konzert Nr. 9 für Violine und Orchester in a-moll in drei verschiedenen Tempi mit professioneller Begleitung erarbeiten. Es handelt sich um eine revidierte Neuausgabe, bei der unter anderem die Solostimme mit Fingersätzen versehen wurde.

Auf der ersten CD (CD A) können Sie zuerst die Konzertversion (Violine mit Orchester) eines jeden Satzes anhören. Nach dem Stimmen Ihres Instrumentes (auf beiden CDs Track 1) kann die musikalische Arbeit beginnen. Zum Üben folgt nun im langsamen (CD A) und mittleren Tempo (CD B) die Klavierbegleitung, wobei im langsamen Tempo die Violine als Orientierung leise im Hintergrund zu hören ist. Anschließend können Sie sich im Originaltempo (CD B) vom Orchester begleiten lassen. Jeder Satz wurde in sinnvolle Übe-Abschnitte unterteilt. Diese können Sie mit Hilfe der in der Solostimme angegebenen Track-Nummern auswählen. Weitere Erklärungen hierzu sowie die Namen der Künstler finden Sie auf der letzten Seite dieser Ausgabe; ausführlichere Informationen können Sie im

Internet unter www.dowani.com nachlesen. Alle eingespielten Versionen wurden live aufgenommen.

Die Fingersätze und Bogenstriche in dieser Ausgabe stammen von dem renommierten Violinpädagogen Herbert Scherz. Er war viele Jahre als Professor für Violine und Violinmethodik an den Musikhochschulen in Luzern und Zürich tätig und unterrichtet seit seiner Pensionierung auch heute noch sehr erfolgreich als Privatlehrer. Seine Schüler haben über 150 Preise bei Violin- und Kammermusikwettbewerben erhalten und viele von ihnen sind inzwischen auf internationaler Ebene sehr erfolgreich. 1985 gründete er die „Ministrings Luzern", ein Ensemble mit Kindern und Jugendlichen bis 16 Jahren, das zahlreiche Konzerte im In- und Ausland gibt.

Wir wünschen Ihnen viel Spaß beim Musizieren mit unseren *DOWANI 3 Tempi Play Along*-Ausgaben und hoffen, dass Ihre Musikalität und Ihr Fleiß Sie möglichst bald bis zur Konzertversion führen werden. Unser Ziel ist es, Ihnen durch Motivation, Freude und Spaß die notwendigen Voraussetzungen für effektives Üben zu schaffen.

Ihr DOWANI Team

Concerto No. 9

for Violin and Orchestra, Op. 104
A minor / la mineur / a-moll

Ch. A. de Bériot (1802 – 1870)

DOW 4501

10

Violin

Concerto No. 9

for Violin and Orchestra, Op. 104
A minor / la mineur / a-moll

I A2

Ch. A. de Bériot (1802 – 1870)
Edited by H. Scherz

DOW 4501

2

II

8

Rondo

9

DOW 4501

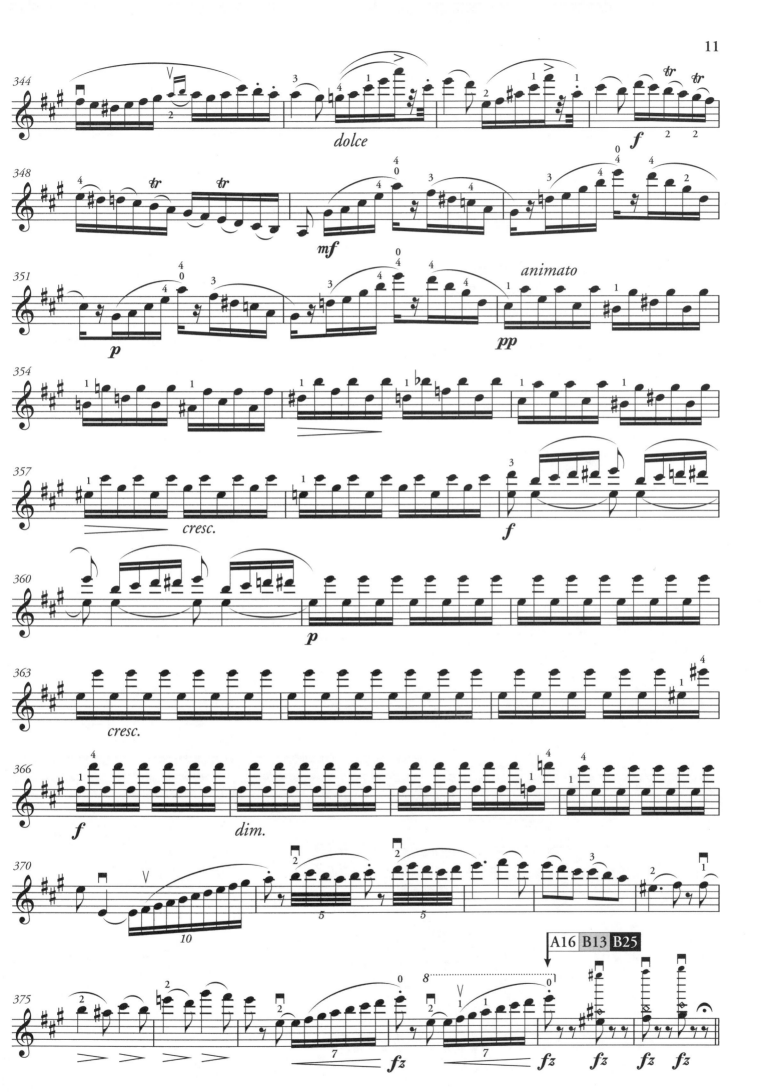

Coda

Più animato

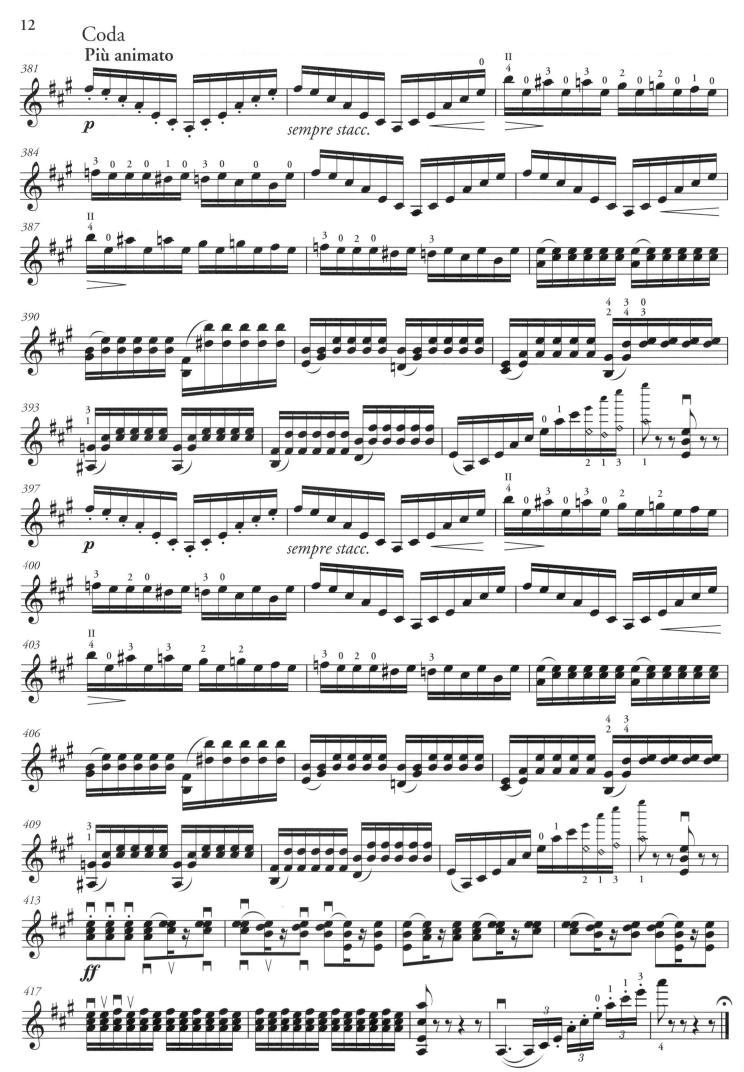

Rondo

Allegretto moderato

Allegretto moderato

Solo

Coda

ENGLISH

DOWANI CD:

- Track No. 1   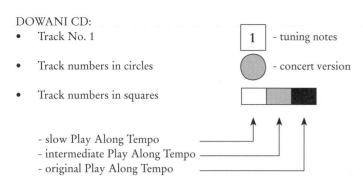 - tuning notes

- Track numbers in circles   - concert version

- Track numbers in squares

     - slow Play Along Tempo
     - intermediate Play Along Tempo
     - original Play Along Tempo

- Additional tracks for longer movements or pieces

- **Double CD:** CD1 = A, CD2 = B

- **Concert version:** violin and orchestra

- **Slow tempo:** piano accompaniment with violin in the background

- **Intermediate tempo:** piano accompaniment only

- **Original tempo:** orchestra only

Please note that the recorded version of the piano accompaniment may di▯ slightly from the sheet music. This is due to the spontaneous character of music making and the artistic freedom of the musicians. The original shee▯ music for the solo part is, of course, not affected.

FRANÇAIS

DOWANI CD :

- Plage N° 1   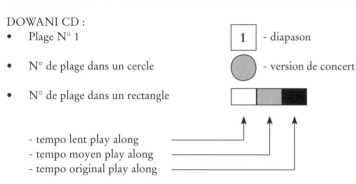 - diapason

- N° de plage dans un cercle   - version de concert

- N° de plage dans un rectangle

     - tempo lent play along
     - tempo moyen play along
     - tempo original play along

- Plages supplémentaires pour mouvements ou morceaux longs

- **Double CD :** CD1 = A, CD2 = B

- **Version de concert :** violon et orchestre

- **Tempo lent :** accompagnement de piano avec violon en fond sonore

- **Tempo moyen :** seulement l'accompagnement de piano

- **Tempo original :** seulement l'accompagnement d'orchestre

L'enregistrement de l'accompagnement de piano peut présenter quelques différences mineures par rapport au texte de la partition. Ceci est du à la liber▯ artistique des musiciens et résulte d'un jeu spontané et vivant, mais n'affecte, bien entendu, d'aucune manière la partie soliste.

DEUTSCH

DOWANI CD:

- Track Nr. 1   - Stimmtöne

- Trackangabe im Kreis   - Konzertversion

- Trackangabe im Rechteck

     - langsames Play Along Tempo
     - mittleres Play Along Tempo
     - originales Play Along Tempo

- Zusätzliche Tracks bei längeren Sätzen oder Stücken

- **Doppel-CD:** CD1 = A, CD2 = B

- **Konzertversion:** Violine und Orchester

- **Langsames Tempo:** Klavierbegleitung mit Violine im Hintergrund

- **Mittleres Tempo:** nur Klavierbegleitung

- **Originaltempo:** nur Orchester

Die Klavierbegleitung auf der CD-Aufnahme kann gegenüber dem Noten▯ kleine Abweichungen aufweisen. Dies geht in der Regel auf die künstlerisc▯ Freiheit der Musiker und auf spontanes, lebendiges Musizieren zurück. D▯ Solostimme bleibt davon selbstverständlich unangetastet.

DOWANI - 3 Tempi Play Along is published by:
DOWANI International Est.
Industriestrasse 24 / Postfach 156, FL-9487 Bendern,
Principality of Liechtenstein
Phone: ++423 370 11 15, Fax ++423 370 19 44
Email: info@dowani.com
www.dowani.com

Recording & Digital Mastering: Pavel Lavrenenkov, Russia
CD-Production: MediaMotion, The Netherlands
Music Notation: Notensatz Thomas Metzinger, Germany
Design: Andreas Haselwanter, Austria
Printed by: Zrinski d.d., Croatia
Made in the Principality of Liechtenstein

Concert Versi
Alexander Trostyansky, Vi▯
Russian Philharmonic Orchestra Mosc▯
Konstantin Krimets, Condu▯

3 Tempi Accompanim▯
Slo
Vitaly Junitsky, Pi▯

Intermedia
Vitaly Junitsky, Pi▯

Origi▯
Russian Philharmonic Orchestra Mosc▯
Konstantin Krimets, Condu▯